LET YOUR LIGHT SHINE,
My Girl.

Turtle Publishing

Copyright © 2025 Lindsay Silvagni

All rights reserved. No part of this publication may be reproduced, stored in or introduced into a retrieval system, or transmitted in any form, or by any means (electronic, mechanical, photocopying, recording or otherwise) without the prior written permission of the author. Any person who does any unauthorised acts in relation to this publication will be liable to criminal prosecution and civil claims for damages. Enquiries should be made through the publisher.

Lindsay Silvagni has asserted her right under the Copyright, Designs and Patents Act 1988 to be identified as the distributor of this work.

First published by Turtle Publishing 2025
Illustrations by Mirjana Segan
Cover by Turtle Publishing

ISBN: 978-1-7643960-3-5 (paperback)
ISBN: 978-1-7643960-6-6 (hardback)

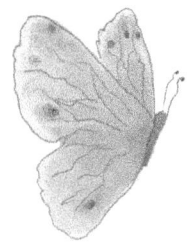

For all the women in my life.

Most notably, my beautiful daughters, Leni and Milla.

This is for you. Life learnt and shared in my words for you.

May you find your light in this world and let it shine.

LET YOUR LIGHT SHINE,

My Girl.

Appreciate your youth.

Enjoy the process of growing.

But don't wish time away in wanting to grow up too fast.

As you get older, you will understand the boundaries that age places upon us.

One of the greatest gifts in life is knowing and understanding the power and the beauty of your youth.

Don't rush.

Hold on to this time. It is beautiful, fleeting and magical.

Endless possibilities lay before you.

Grab it, and

Let your light shine,

Love your body.

LOVE your body. Truly, wholly, unapologetically.

Fuel it with the good stuff but don't berate yourself when you indulge in the bad stuff.

Don't be concerned with what other people think of it.

Don't concern yourself with negative thoughts towards your body. Release the grip of your own criticism.

Celebrate all it can do, even if it places restrictions at times.

Your body is yours and it is the greatest gift you'll ever own.

Speak to your body as if it is someone you love.

Be kind to it, and
Let your light shine, My Girl.

Celebrate your success.

BUT celebrate the success and abundance of those around you too.

Never think that others have more than you. That they are better than you. Never think that you are missing out.

Jealousy is destructive.

A quiet thief that creeps in and convinces you that your worth is less.

Remember, we are all on our own path in life. Sometimes we feel behind and sometimes we feel ahead.

Don't get caught up in comparing yourself to others. It will only lead to disappointment, most likely with yourself.

Cheer fiercely for others. Cheer fiercely for yourself.

Learn to be content, and
Let your light shine, My Girl.

Fill your cup.

Fill your cup with kindness.

It is a superpower.

Spread it far and wide, without fear of consequence.

Don't be disrespectful to others.

Don't let others be disrespectful to you.

Its okay to stand up for yourself. To stand tall, to honour yourself.

Enable yourself to fill your soul from within.

But remember, doing something for others is the most rewarding of all.

Be of service. Lift others up.

Share your truth, share your vulnerabilities, and Let your light shine, My Girl.

Find your people.

The most honest friendships are those where you can be exactly who you are without judgement.

Find friendships like that.

And in return, hold space for others to feel that same safety with you.

Don't be fooled by others or fool others into believing you're something that you're not.

It never ends well.

A true friend is the one you can laugh with, cry with. Time may pass you by from a distance, but when in each other's presence, it's like no time has passed at all.

They are the sacred ones.

Trust in them, relish in them, and
Let your light shine, My Girl.

Open your heart.

Open yourself to the limitless possibilities of love and being loved in return.

Don't be reckless with other people's hearts, and in turn, don't let others be reckless with yours.

Heartbreak is real. Heartbreak is raw. Heartbreak is a blessing...most of the time.

Sometimes you don't know how strong you are until you go through the unimaginable suffering of a broken heart.

There is always a lesson to be learnt.

Love flows from an endless well; don't let past heartbreak keep you from opening your heart again.

If in doubt, love more. The heart is like a balloon; the more it expands, the more chance it has to fly.

Breathe in love; it is the best feeling in the entire world.

Love hard.

Love wholeheartedly.

Love always, and

Let your light shine, My Girl.

Notice your breath.

Deep breaths are little love notes to your body. A gentle reminder that you are safe. That you are here. That this moment is enough.

It is in the stillness that time pauses, that moment where everything stops. You are not reaching for the past. You are not racing to the future. You are simply being, here and now.

Be present.

Make space for mindfulness.

Take time to be gentle with yourself.

Worrying only lets you use your imagination to create things that you don't want, to create fear.

Thoughts are not facts.

Your mind will believe what you feed it.

So, feed it love.

Feed it hope.

Feed it truth, and

Let your light shine, My Girl.

Trust your worth.

Indulge in your capabilities.

Don't be deceived by beauty and what it means to be beautiful.

Beauty is not a filtered image you see on the screen. It's not the shape of your face or the length of your hair. It's not the outline of your body or the label on your clothes.

What is beautiful? YOU are beautiful.

Your strength. Your bravery. Your courage. Your resilience. Your kindness. Your compassion. Your innocence. Your heart.

That is beautiful.

Share it with the world, and

Let your light shine, My Girl.

My Girl, always remember.

Imagine freely.

Dream with an open heart.

Love with all your being.

Believe anything is possible.

And the truth is...it is.

Walk your path with courage, and

Let your light shine, My Girl.

www.ingramcontent.com/pod-product-compliance
Lightning Source LLC
Chambersburg PA
CBHW061212070526
44583CB00025B/3227